SAFETY SUPERHEROES

STAYING SAFE ON THE ROAD

THERESA EMMINIZER

PowerKiDS press

Published in 2024 by The Rosen Publishing Group, Inc.
2544 Clinton Street, Buffalo, NY 14224

First Edition

Editor: Theresa Emminizer
Book Design: Rachel Rising

Photo Credits: Cover, p. 1 Irina Wilhauk/Shutterstock.com; pp. 4, 6, 8, 10, 12, 14, 16, 18, 20 anndypit/Shutterstock.com; p. 5 Prostock-studio/Shutterstock.com; p. 7 Tom Wang/Shutterstock.com; p. 9 Taras Grebinets/Shutterstock.com; p. 11 Lopolo/Shutterstock.com; p. 13 MNStudio/Shutterstock.com; p. 15 Pixel-Shot/Shutterstock.com; p. 17 Pat Shrader/Shutterstock.com; p. 19 Sergey Ryzhov/Shutterstock.com; p. 21 Norenko Andrey/Shutterstock.com.

Library of Congress Cataloging-in-Publication Data

Names: Emminizer, Theresa.
Title: Staying safe on the road / Theresa Emminizer.
Description: New York : Powerkids Press, 2024. | Series: Safety superheroes | Includes glossary and index.
Identifiers: ISBN 9781642826050 (pbk.) | ISBN 9781642826067 (library bound) | ISBN 9781642826074 (ebook)
Subjects: LCSH: Traffic safety–Juvenile literature. | Pedestrians–Safety measures–Juvenile literature. | Safety education–Juvenile literature.
Classification: LCC HE5614.E46 2024 | DDC 363.12'5–dc23

Manufactured in the United States of America

CPSIA Compliance Information: Batch #CSPK24. For Further Information contact Rosen Publishing at 1-800-237-9932.

CONTENTS

Stay Safe!

It's great to get out and go places! But the road can be a **dangerous** place. Whether you're driving in the car, riding your bike, or going for a walk, it's important to follow safety rules. You can be a safety superhero on the road!

In the Car

Buckle up! Always wear your seatbelt while riding in the car. Never put your hands, feet, head, or any other part of your body outside the car window. Don't open your door while the car is moving. Stay in your seat.

When riding in the car, it's important not to **distract** the driver. Noisy or wild behavior can make it hard for the driver to **concentrate** and may even cause an accident! Never yell or throw things in the car.

On Your Bike

Wear a helmet every time you ride your bike, even if you're only going a short way! A helmet will keep your head safe. Keep both hands on your bike's handlebars. Don't ride your bike barefoot. Wear sneakers or shoes that cover your toes.

Wear light or bright colored clothes when you ride your bike. This helps cars see you! Never ride after dark. Don't listen to music or wear headphones when riding. Listen for cars. Follow the rules of the road.

Going for a Walk

It's best not to walk by yourself. Go with a friend or somebody in your family! Don't talk to **strangers**. If a stranger comes up to you or asks you for help, don't talk to them. Walk away to a safe place.

Be careful when crossing the street. Never run across the middle of the road. Go to an **intersection** where there are traffic lights. Stop, look, and listen for cars. Wait for the walk sign to come on.

Rules of the Road

Just like a driver, you need to follow the rules of the road. Stop at stop signs. Follow traffic lights. Red means stop. Green means go. Yellow means slow down. Be careful of cars on the street, in parking lots, and in driveways.

You're a Safety Superhero!

You can help make the road a safer place. Follow the rules of the road. Look and listen carefully when you're walking or biking. Be a helpful rider in the car. You can be a safety superhero!

GLOSSARY

concentrate: To think about or focus on something.

dangerous: Unsafe.

distract: Make it hard for someone to concentrate.

intersection: A place with traffic lights where two roads meet.

stranger: Someone you don't know.

FOR MORE INFORMATION

BOOKS

Schuette, Sarah L. *Staying Safe! Bike Safety*. Rocheport, MO: Pebble Publishing, 2019.

Schuette, Sarah L. *Staying Safe! Pedestrian Safety*. Rocheport, MO: Pebble Publishing, 2019.

WEBSITES

Kids Health
kidshealth.org/en/kids/bike-safety.html
Find out more about bike safety.

Safety 4 Kids
www.safety4kids.com.au/safety-zone_road-safety
Learn more ways to stay safe on the road.

Publisher's note to educators and parents: Our editors have carefully reviewed these websites to ensure that they are suitable for students. Many websites change frequently, however, and we cannot guarantee that a site's future contents will continue to meet our high standards of quality and educational value. Be advised that students should be closely supervised whenever they access the internet.

INDEX